Maldives Travel Guide

Sightseeing, Hotel, Restaurant & Shopping Highlights

Gary Jennings

Table of Contents

Maldives..6
   Culture..8
   Location & Orientation 9
   Climate & When to Visit..10

Sightseeing Highlights..12
   Male 12
      Jumhooree Maidan 13
      Esjehi Gallery...13
      Mulee-Aage Palace..14
      Tomb of Mohammad Thakurufaanu.....................15
      National Museum...15
      Grand Friday Mosque (Huskuru Miskiiy)............16
   Surfing in the Maldives 17
      Male Atoll...18
      Central Atolls 19
      Outer Atolls...19
   Scuba Diving 19
      Banana Reef Diving..20
      Other Notable Diving Locations............................21
      Shipwreck Diving...22
   Atoll Cruising & Live-Aboard Holidays.....................22
   Environmental Tourism 24
   Kudahuvadhoo Island 24

Recommendations for the Budget Traveller...........26
   Places to Stay..26
      Hotel Octave..28
      Asdu Sun Island 28
      Lucky Hiya Hotel 29
      Fuana Inn...29
      Boutique Inn at Villa Shabnamee.........................30
   Places to Eat..30
      Sea House Maldives...31
      Symphony Restaurant...32
      Chop Chop 32
      Seagull Cafe House..33

Shell Beans 33
Places to Shop **34**
Chaandanee Magu 34
Dhoni Boats, Shark's Teeth & Maldivian Curiosities 35
Creative Arts & Crafts Training Center 36
Reed Mats of Huvadhoo 37
Wooden Boxes from Thulhaadhoo 37

Maldives

Beautifully situated in the Indian Ocean to the south of the Indian subcontinent, the Maldives is a group of over a thousand tiny islands and atolls. Offering its visitors luxurious pampering combined with peace and seclusion, the Maldive islands are a popular romantic destination for newlyweds and other holidaymakers.

Allow your mind to imagine a day on one of the Maldives. You are on a small tropical island far away from the hustle and bustle of the daily rat race. On a sandy atoll set in turquoise waters with coconut palm trees waving in the gentle breeze.

Resort staff on the Maldives pride themselves on catering to the individual wishes of their guests. You can even procure the services of your own personal butler.

The tourism industry of the Maldives has traditionally focused on the islands exclusive five star resorts but has started to offer alternatives for the more budget-conscious and independent traveler.

There are over a hundred resorts in the Maldives. There are two main types, the beach bungalow and the water bungalow. The thatched water villas are stilt-mounted over lagoons and linked by wooden walkways. While this enhances an atmosphere of privacy, the downside is that you should be prepared to do a fair amount of strolling to and from other facilities on the island. Resort stay minimizes contact with the local population and often confines the tourist to one island.

Resorts and structured cruises often include accommodation, meals, facilities, gear and activities such as diving or surfing as a combined package. While the price tag may seem quite high at first glance, it often presents good value for money if you add up how much the individual components of the holiday would have cost you.

In some parts of the Maldives, the perception remains that all visitors are wealthy and some individual services are overpriced and exploitative. As the Maldives covers a large portion of sea, policing resources are spread thin in certain sectors, making some parts of the Maldives safer than others. All these factors should be born in mind when considering an independent holiday experience.

Culture

According to historians, the islands of the Maldives have been occupied since the 4th century BC, with its people including a mixture of natives from Arabia, India and East Africa. The traditional dhoni boats used for sea travel speak of the islands Arabian influence, but it is believed that the original inhabitants were fishermen, of Dravidian descent.

The official language of the Maldives is Dhivehi, which is related to Sinhala, the language of Sri Lanka, but with smatterings of Arabic as well as two Indian languages, namely Hindi and Urdu. English is widely used and at some resorts, staff members are also fluent in languages like German or Italian.

The local population is largely Islamic and Muslim holidays are observed. This impacts on its holiday facilities in a number of ways. While resorts often opt for a more relaxed interpretation of local customs, it means that some of the islands, particularly those with a significant local population, are 'dry' - in other words, no alcohol is served or sold. Resorts that have the exclusive use of a certain island are usually allowed to sell alcohol. The so-called 'dry' islands often boast an unusually wide selection of non-alcoholic alternatives.

The predominance of Islam also means that, while the dress code may be relaxed on independent resort islands, it can be quite strict where Maldivians reside. Do not flaunt your skimpiest bikini on public beaches, if you wish to avoid trouble with the local authorities.

Although the Maldives is seen primarily as a place of leisure, the nation has produced a few widely respected brains in various fields. Hassan Ugail, born in Hithadhoo in the Maldives, went on to become one of the youngest professors of science at the University of Bradford in the UK. His subjects are mathematics and computer science. Prominent writers from the Maldives include Ibrahim Shihab and Muhammad Jameel Didi, who penned the words to the National Anthem. A music group from the Maldives, Zero Degree Atoll, has recorded three albums and performed in several locations in Europe. Their music utilizes natural and traditional sounds, and relies heavily on cultural influences.

Location & Orientation

The Maldives is an archipelago of around 1100 tiny islands, arranged in 26 atolls and located just above the equator. Its extended territory stretches across 500 km and its nearest neighbors are India to the North and Sri Lanka to the Northeast.

Although the Maldives represents the smallest land area and population of Asia, it covers a territory of over 90,000 square km. It is the lowest country in the world. Its highest point, in the Addu Atoll is only 2.17m above sea level.

There is an international airport on Male, the capital and it receives frequent flights from Colombo, Sri Lanka, Thiruvananthapuram in the Indian state of Kerala, Dubai and Kuala Lumpur. The airport is usually lined with seaplane Air Taxis, ready to transport arrivals to the individual island of their stay. These typically have a capacity of about 20 passengers. Depending on the island, a seaplane transfer can set you back a few hundred dollars. For example, a flight to the Baa Atoll costs around $356. The alternative is a transfer by speedboat.

Climate & When to Visit

The Maldives basks in a tropical climate all year round, enjoying warm sunshine and frequent tropical showers of rain. During the period between May and November, you can experience a high degree of humidity, frequent rain and a fair amount of wind. The climate is drier between December and April, but accommodation rates can be double during this period, especially over Christmas and New Year.

Surfers should know that the Maldives experiences the best waves from March to May and also September to November. The optimum time for diving is between January and April. The weather can be unstable in May and June and cloud cover can be a complication until September. While the weather conditions suitable for diving improve from October, an abundance of plankton may compromise visibility in the water during October and November. Windy conditions may be experienced in December.

The low season, when rates are cheaper, occurs between May and November. The water displays remarkable clarity in April and also November which make these periods attractive for diving enthusiasts. The peak season is between December and January and in the months of February, March, and also August.

Sightseeing Highlights

Male

Male had always been known as the King's Island and remains the capital and head of administration in the Maldives. It is also a fully urbanized hub of commercial activity and home to almost one third of the combined population of the Maldives. Male boasts several tourist attractions of note, a shopping district and a number of hotels and restaurants. It is near the airport and as well as a number of resorts.

Jumhooree Maidan

The waterfront area of Male, known as Jumhooree Maidan, was first laid out in 1989 and has since become a popular, trendy meeting place for both locals and foreign visitors. The square, also known as Republic Square, includes the Presidential jetty and the National Security Service and the Police are headquartered here. Another attraction is the Islamic Center on the southern side, which is part of the Grand Friday Mosque. The western side features a number of commercial buildings and another attractive feature, is the plantation along the shore. The square is often used as a venue for cultural and other special events. On those occasions special decorative lighting is often evident. Teenagers love to hang out on Jumhooree Maidan in the evenings.

Esjehi Gallery

The building that houses the Esjehi Gallery dates back to 1870 and had originally belonged to a man of high rank. Although compact, it includes some beautiful woodwork and carving details and hosts a mixture of traditional and contemporary works of art, some of which may be available for purchase. It is located east of Sultan Park and near several restaurants. Bear in mind that it is closed till 2pm on Fridays.

Mulee-Aage Palace

Opposite the Friday Mosque, Male

The palace was constructed almost 100 years ago, between 1914 and 1919 under the supervision of Sultan Mohamed Shamsuddeen III. It is an impressive structure with imposing iron gates and beautiful architecture based on the Colonial era of Ceylon.

Originally dedicated to the Sultan's son and heir, it was constructed on the site of a prior ancestral home, but never served as Royal Palace. That honor had belonged to Sultan Park, where the National Museum is now located. The young prince, Hassan Uzziddin did use Mulee-Aage for regular concerts and other social activities between 1920 and 1934 and this led to a smear campaign against his rule, led by his own uncle. He was banished in 1936.

During the Second World War, the garden was utilized to cultivate fruit and vegetables. In 1953, Ibrahim Nasir adopted the building as his Presidential Palace. Queen Elizabeth II of England had stayed at Mulee-Aage during a visit to the Maldives.

Tomb of Mohammad Thakurufaanu

Al-Sultan Ghazi Muhammad Bodu Thakurufaanu is one of the heroes of Maldivian history. Born and raised on Utheemu, his favorite activity as a young boy had been taming birds, but as he grew up, he was troubled by the harsh rule of the Portuguese sponsored regime in Male. He rose to power on his native island and began the campaign for the overthrow of King Andreas Andreas, the Portuguese ruler. After liberating the Maldives, he ruled as sultan from 1573 to 1585.

The victory of Muhammad Thakurufaanu is celebrated as a National Day on the first of the month Rabi' al-awwal, according to the Islamic calendar. The tomb occupies the compound of Bihuroazu Kamanaa Miskiiy. It is an elegant monument in white, surrounded by a tranquil setting at the center of Male.

National Museum

Sultan Park, Male
Tel: 960 332 2254

The National Museum first opened its doors in 1952 and is located in Sultan Park, formerly part of the Royal Palace Compound in Male. The collections include costumes, clothes, royal artefacts, boat models, ceremonial chairs and many more objects from more opulent times.

The museum also had several relics from the pre-Islamic Buddhist era, but nearly all of these had been destroyed in a recent attack by religious extremists. The park contains a 'wish tree', which is believed to grant wishes to anyone who touches it.

Grand Friday Mosque (Huskuru Miskiiy)

Built around 1656 by Sultan Ibrahim Iskandhar, the Grand Friday Mosque can accommodate up to 5000 worshippers in one sitting and has priceless art treasures. Some of the architectural features include a golden dome, coral engravings and decorative minarets. The materials include a mixture of coral and various types of wood such as teak, redwood and sandalwood. The carvings featured in the interior are particularly exquisite.

The building is regarded as a National Treasure, several Sultans and other important figures from the past of the Maldives are buried here. The Grand Friday Mosque, also known as the Huskuru Miskyii or Masjid-al Sultan Mohamed Thakurufaanu-al-A'z'am, contains the Islamic Center, a facility that has hosted seminars on an international scale. Do bear in mind that, since it is a place of devotion, visitors are required to cover up.

Surfing in the Maldives

There is an interesting story to the origins of surfing in the Maldives. It all began in 1973, when two Australian surfers, Tony Hinde and Mark Scanlon were shipwrecked in the Maldives. During their extended stay to repair their ship, Hinde discovered the surfing potential and decided to settle in the Maldives. He converted to Islam, married a local woman and invited fellow surfers to visit. For years, the surfer's paradise remained a well-guarded secret, within a small circle of surfing enthusiasts. During the 1980s, he began offering private surfing tours and formed Atoll Adventures, which partnered with an Australian tour operator. His excursions were based around the Thari Village resort, now known as the Chaaya Island Dhonveli, where a near perfect wave swell occurs on a southern beach known as Pasta Point. The site now hosts international surfing events.

If you wish to enjoy the surf in the Maldives, but do not quite want to book an exclusive tour, there are several spots to visit for the best waves. The first thing you should bear in mind is that there are different optimum surfing periods for different parts of the island group. From February through to April, the Outer Atolls should be visited for the best waves. The North Male Atoll enjoys the best wave action from April to October, while the Central Atolls experience the most suitable waves from May to April.

Male Atoll

There is a Surf Camp at Cokes that is operated by the Australian Brian James and his business partner Chiharu Kanno from Japan. Also known as Cokes Inn, because of its close proximity to the Coca-Cola factory in the Maldives, the establishment offers a package that includes accommodation and full board and facilities surf board hire, dinghy transport to other nearby surfing locations as well as diving and scuba equipment if you feel like a change. Do bear in mind that Cokes Inn as well as the rest of the island is 'dry', meaning that no alcohol is allowed.

Cokes and another location known among surfing enthusiasts as Chickens both enjoys swells of up to 3m. The beach at Cokes is partially sheltered from southerly winds that may affect the wind, resulting in the hollowest waves in the Maldives. Chickens boasts two major advantages. The wave frequency is among the fastest in the region and a ride at Chickens can extend up to 500m before it breaks. Other surfing locations in the North Atoll region include Ninjas, Honkys, Sultans, Tombstones and Jailbreaks.

Along South Male, you will discover popular surf beaches such as Riptides, Kate's, Natives, Twin Peaks, Towns and Gurus.

Central Atolls

If you wish to avoid the crowds, and which serious surfer does not, you may wish to explore some of the surf spots to be found along the Central Atolls. This region is located between the Male Atolls and the Outer Atolls and includes beaches such as Veyvah, Mulhah, Muli Outside and Muli Inside, all of which can be found on the eastern coast of the Mulaku Atoll. The southern coast of the Hadhdhunmathee Atoll also enjoys great wave action. Recommended locations include Mundoo, Yin-Yang, Isdhoo, Gaadhoo and Maabaidhoo.

Outer Atolls

The Outer Atolls are more remote, but there are well-organized cruises that target this region. Some of the surfing locations here include Beacons, Castaways, Tigers, Five Islands, Two Ways, Blue Bowls, Rockets, Love Charms and Booga Reef. Beacons and Love Charms have seen swells of up to 3m. Bear in mind that this section of the Maldives enjoys a different peak season.

Scuba Diving

The Maldives is highly recommended for underwater exploration and there is much to explore. An abundance of varied marine life live on or near the coral reefs and lagoons of the area. A popular attraction is the Manta Ray, of which an estimated 10,000 can be found in or around the Maldives.

They are the rock stars of the coral reefs, often parking themselves near a reef at a so-called 'cleaning station', where smaller fish would swarm their bodies in search of dead tissue or parasites to devour. The activity presents a win-win situation for both the smaller fish and the manta ray, and provides a wonderful spectacle for divers to observe. Manta rays are amiable, tranquil creatures that do not mind being observed by human visitors, so long as they are not disturbed.

Other fish are admired simply for their beauty. The schools of blue-line snappers, parrotfish, butterfly fish, clownfish, triggerfish and oriental sweetlips make ornamental and ever moving features against a backdrop of coral. Other inhabitants of Malidivian waters include the barracuda, the long-nose hawk-fish, the Napoleon wrasse, powder-blue surgeonfish, the white-lined lionfish, the square-tail coral grouper, the saddled puffer fish, the reef shark, the whale shark, the honeycomb moray and the somewhat elusive eagle ray and stingray. The Maldives represents an ecosystem of over 700 different species of fish and other marine life. Various species of turtles also live in the waters around the Maldives and some nest on its beaches.

Banana Reef Diving

Banana Reef was the original site that popularised diving in the Maldives. It boasts several notable features such as a pinnacle and various overhangs and the coral growth is vibrant and prolific. The name refers to the shape of the shallow reef, which lies in the Giftun Strait, North Male Atoll.

There are several caves worth exploring at Banana Reef and some of these feature exotic inhabitants. You can hope to see squirrelfish, soldierfish, bannerfish, pufferfish, Oriental Sweetlips, several species of wrasse and fusilier. Since the site entertains such frequent visitors from divers, some its resident fish have grown quite tame in the presence of human company.

Other Notable Diving Locations

Cocoa Corner in the Male Atoll is a popular site for divers wishing to see sharks. It can be explored from different directions and there is a good chance that you may be able to view juvenile Grey Reef sharks. Other inhabitants include schools of jackfish as well as Eagle rays. Located in the North Ari Atoll, Dhonkalho Tila is well known as a 'cleaning station' for the manta rays. It also features an interesting system of whirlpools and tidal currents. Divers usually choose the channel connecting Maalhos with Himendhoo. Another favorite hangout of the charismatic manta rays is Hukrueli Faru. Other recommended sites in the North Male region include Lion's Head, Kudu Haa, Middle Point, Girifushi Thila, Sunlight Thila, Okobe Thila and Nassimo Thila.

Although the Broken Rock diving site features some unusual overhangs and coral formations, the strong currents can be treacherous, making it suitable only for experienced divers with the right back-up gear. Other sites recommended only for advanced divers are Gangehi Kandu, and Maalhos Thila, both of which can be found in the North Ari Atoll.

Shipwreck Diving

There are a few diving sites in the Maldives where you can hope to encounter more than coral, sharks, rays and reef fish. In the North Ari Atoll to the southwest of Fesdhoo Island, you could explore the wreck of a 30m fishing vessel. Besides the ship, you can also hope to see a number of interesting species such as grouper, moray eels, jackfish, lionfish, butterfly fish, reef sharks and hammerheads. Sponges, feather stars, various types of coral and other opportunistic creatures have colonized the sides of the wreck.

Another dive site featuring a shipwreck can be found in the North Male Atoll near Hulhule Airport Island. The *Maldives Victory*, a 110m cargo vessel, went down in February 1982 and has since gotten a new lease of life as the home of abundant schools of grouper, tuna and fusilier as well as families of turtles. Divers to the site should beware to avoid the jagged damaged edges of the wreck.

Atoll Cruising & Live-Aboard Holidays

There is an alternate option available for visitors who are reluctant to confine themselves to a single island. Various types of Atoll cruises will allow you the opportunity to experience different parts of the Maldives from the comfort of an air-conditioned cabin with accommodation, all meals and on board entertainment included in the price.

There are general and specialized packages. One type of tour might focus on finding and stopping at the best surfing beaches. Another could take you to some truly unusual diving or fishing locations.

To a degree, the experience can be personalized, if you wish to visit a local village or book a spa treatment, but these requests will need to be made in advance. Although food, tea, coffee and snacks are included in the price, alcohol is usually charged separately.

In some cases, the arrangement can be between a group of at least eight co-travellers, who may enjoy a fair amount of control over the itinerary at between $195 and $260 per person. A more structured cruise could cost between $1210 and $1390 per week.

These cruise boats, also known as live-aboards, feature many of the same conveniences you would expect from a hotel stay such as air-conditioning, television, a bar, en-suite bathroom and even Internet access. One great package is offered by the live-aboard, **Carina**, which features a typical daily rate might be $175 per day, a fare that would include three meals. Another live-aboard, the **MV Orion**, is a bit pricier at $299 per night, but offers luxuries such as the use of a Jacuzzi, satellite phone, Internet, a library and first aid facilities. The ship also features its own desalination plant. Do bear in mind that different cruise packages follow routes through different sections of the Maldives.

Environmental Tourism

There are a few resorts that offer specialized services that might be worth investigating. With a strong emphasis on preserving and protecting the environment, the Banyan Tree Global Foundation established a Marine Lab on Vabbinfaru in 2004 and its success led to a second facility in 2007. The island of Velavaru in the South Nilandhe Atoll is home to a Marine Lab that studies various ecological concerns such as coral growth, sharks and the green turtles that still reside in this region. Other activities include dolphin monitoring, which is undertaken in partnership with the World Wildlife Fund.

Guests that stay at the nearby Angsana Velavaru resort can participate in one of the facility's projects - the planting of new coral gardens. The resort also offers marine biology classes and guided snorkelling safaris. Angsana Velavaru is a known nesting site for the Green Turtle and the Hawksbill Turtle, both of which enjoy the protection of the Marine Lab. The Green Turtle is reckoned to be a keystone species, meaning that their presence facilitates the survival of several other species. Although the coral reefs are delicate, they support 25 percent of the marine life of the Maldives. Guests of the resort have assisted in the creation of four new coral gardens in the region.

Kudahuvadhoo Island

Islam dominates the Maldives today, but until the 12th century, most of the region's people were Buddhists. It is believed that the religion came to the Maldives from nearby Sri Lanka.

Most of the earliest writing, architecture and art speak of Buddhist influence. Kudahuvadhoo Island in the South Nilande Atoll is of particular interest as it features a mound, known as a "hawitta", which conceals the ruins of a Buddhist temple. Other attractions of the island include the old mosque of Kudahuvadhoo, which boasts particularly fine masonry detail. The island also has excellent diving facilities. It is located about 20 minutes away from the airport, by speedboat. The Scandinavian explorer Thor Heyerdahl visited the island in the 1980s.

Recommendations for the Budget Traveller

Places to Stay

For many years, the development of tourism in the Maldives has focused largely on self-contained resorts. Such resorts often have exclusive access to all the tourist facilities on a small island.

At the high-end of the market, a stay in the Maldives could set you back between $700 and $1400 a night. Even more modest resorts can cost between $200 and $500 a night.

In exchange, the service is often top-notch and highly personalized. Nearly all resorts offer packages that include meals and sometimes even drinks, although alcohol may be charged separately, if allowed. Do bear in mind that an airport transfer to one of the outlying atolls can be quite expensive.

Resorts offer a greater degree of privacy and security than a stay within the capital or some of the more urbanized areas of the Maldives. Here are a few tips for saving money. Beach bungalows are generally cheaper than water bungalows. A few resorts that may be a little easier on your budget are Embudu Village (tel. 960 664-0063) located on a tiny island by the same name near Hulule airport, where rates begin at $140 a night, Kuramathi Resort (tel. 960 666-0527), where accommodation begins at $175 a night and Club Rannalhi, Adaaran (tel. 960 664-0376), located in the South Male Atoll, where accommodation begins at $175 a night.

Another possibility is to book a voyage aboard one of several live-aboard cruisers. This will allow you to see more of the Maldives and will cover accommodation and meals. Since independent transport options in the Maldives can be extremely expensive, this form of holiday can cut costs in several ways. If you wish to base yourself in the capital, there are a number of choices for accommodation.

Hotel Octave

Kaaminee Magu, Jan'buma
Male
Tel: 960 3013030
http://www.hotel-octave-maldives.com/

Located just a few minutes from the Main Street, this hotel provides an affordable stay right in the heart of the capital of the Maldives. Rooms are small, but well maintained and equipped with conveniences such as air-conditioning, flat screen television, shower, a well-stocked mini-fridge and a work desk with Wifi coverage. The hotel also has a restaurant, which serves a medley of Maldivian, Indian, Asian and Western cuisine. Accommodation begins at $80 a night and breakfast is included.

Asdu Sun Island

North Atoll
Tel: 960 779 4780
http://www.asdu.com/introduction.htm

A Maldives Island stay usually involves a high degree of pampering at the resort spa, but if instead you wish to enjoy a return to nature at a location ideal for diving and underwater exploration, do consider the Asdu Sun Island.

The facilities are fairly basic, but rooms are spacious and the stay affordable. The resort offers canoeing, water-skiing, snorkelling, windsurfing and volleyball. The resort's diving center offers safe and professional tuition, but this is charged separately.

Internet access is available, as well as the use of a library. Accommodation begins at $70 to $140 for two sharing a double room, but includes all meals.

Lucky Hiya Hotel

H.Homa, Dhonhuraa Goalhi, Male
http://www.luckyhiyahotel.com/

The Lucky Hiya Hotel offers you a base within the capital of the Maldives, but access to island hopping tours and surfing and diving packages. The city itself offers great opportunities for shopping, dining out and exploring some of the Maldivian history. Each room offers the convenience of air conditioning, cable TV and Internet access. There is a laundry service as well as a restaurant on the premises. Accommodation begins at $67 a night.

Fuana Inn

Hulhumale' Beach Road Plot No.10107, Hulhumale

Hulhumalé is a fairly new development that has been conceived on an artificial island in the southern part of the North Male Atoll. Currently it is still under utilized, but it does offer some great value for money, in terms of holiday accommodation.

Furnishings are basic but comfortable and rooms include air-conditioning, television and free high speed Internet. There are snorkelling and diving facilities and a ferry every thirty minutes connects Hulhumale to Male. Expect to pay around $90 per night. This includes breakfast, but as with many hotels and resorts, full board, which includes all meals, can be arranged.

Boutique Inn at Villa Shabnamee

G.Villa Shabnamee, Handhuvarudhey Goalhi, Male 20101

While secluded from the hustle and bustle of the city, the Boutique Inn at Villa Shabnamee is nevertheless conveniently near to the shops and restaurants of central Male, as well as the main transit jetties. The hotel is wheel chair friendly and has a rooftop pool and restaurant. Rooms include television, air conditioning and free Internet access. Accommodation begins at $69 a night and includes breakfast.

Places to Eat

Depending on the type of holiday you choose, you might not even need to look at a restaurant while holidaying in the Maldives. Most resorts and cruises include full or half board in their fare. Full board includes all meals while half board covers breakfast and a dinner buffet. Another choice is all-inclusive, which means that your drinks tab is also part of the package.

There are, however, other dining options. If money is no obstacle and you are looking for a rare dining experience in the Maldives, you may wish to stop at the Ithaa Undersea Restaurant on Rangali Island, where you can admire the marine life through the transparent glass roof. Beware, though. You are looking as at a price tag of around $350 per person without the drinks!

Sea House Maldives

Boduthakurufaanu Magu, 2nd Floor Hulhumale Male'
Ferry Terminal, Male 20005
Tel: 960 3332957

The Sea House offers beautiful views of the ocean all round as you dine on a variety of Asian and Continental dishes. Some of the menu items include pizza, sandwiches, wraps, pasta, fried rice, spicy fajitas, white fish curry, beef stroganoff and fish kebabs. Recommended beverages include carrot juice with ginger, mint lemonade and ginger beer. No alcohol is served. The restaurant does offer free Wifi. Menu prices are offered in the local currency and in US dollars. Expect to pay between $5 and $16. The venue occasionally hosts live music and other social events.

Symphony Restaurant

Athamaa Goalhi, Male
Tel: 960 3326277

Located off Majeedee Magu, Symphony offers a combination of Chinese, Asian and International fare. Menu items include grilled cuttlefish with vegetables, Tuna Macaroni, Fried Rice and Prawn cocktails among the starters. The restaurant has a great selection of vegetarian choices. Symphony Restaurant also delivers. Expect to pay between $8 and $20.

Chop Chop

M. Varunulaa, Aaburuzu Hingun, Male 20213
Tel: 960 331-2407
http://www.eatchopchop.com/

The menu at Chop Chop spans across the different cultural influences that make up the Maldives. Expect to pay just over $5 for Fried Fish and Chips or a chicken chow mein, $4.95 for a spicy chicken wrap, a chicken schnitzel wrap, a chicken schnitzel and chips or a spicy fish wrap, $4.50 for a vegetable fried rice and $5.60 for a stir-fried prawn noodle salad. There are bulk deals such as the full herb-grilled chicken for $12.50 and a half dozen portion of chicken kebabs for $10.45. A portion of chips will cost $2.30 and another mouth-watering snack, the fried momo, or dumplings can be ordered in chicken momo or regular momo, for $3.25 per half dozen.

Seagull Cafe House

Fareedhee Magu, Male
Tel: 332 3332
http://www.seagullmaldives.com/cafe/

Located in a beautiful outdoor setting, the Seagull Cafe is a pleasant place to relax and recharge. The most popular menu item has to be the ice cream, which is available in a wide range of flavors, including strawberry, bubblegum, mint, mango, coffee, hazelnut, kiwi, cherry, melon, pineapple, banana, raspberry, blackberry, vanilla, chocolate, caramel and combinations thereof. Among the beverages, there is a large selection of juices, coffees, milkshakes and other soft drinks. The Seagull Cafe also serves breakfasts and light lunches, featuring items such as grilled cheese sandwich, shrimp tempura, fish and chips, eggs benedict and more. Prices are reasonable and the portions very generous.

Shell Beans

Boduthakurufaanu Magu, Male

The first floor balcony at Shell Beans offers an excellent view of the ferry terminal below. The menu includes a variety of home made sandwiches, of which chicken tikka is a favorite, pastries such as cheesecake and Danish, pizzas and salad. The venue also includes free Wifi coverage.

Places to Shop

You should bear a few things in mind, when doing business and shopping in the Maldives. As the locals are used to the type of tourists that frequent five star resorts, some of them have few scruples about charging overly-exorbitant prices. Due to environmental policies, the trade and export on certain items are restricted. These include goods made of coral, turtle and tortoise shell. An added convenience in some locations is a type of mobile bazaar, which offers crafts to visitors. Most shops in the tourist areas are open till 11pm, but may be closed on Fridays till 2pm.

Chaandanee Magu

Male

The Maldives is not particularly well known for its shopping opportunities. Most tourists visit for other reasons and many of the resorts are self-contained to such an extent that guests hardly need to venture beyond the resort confines for any reason. The closest the island group has to offer in terms of a shopping district can be found along Chaandanee Magu in the capital of Male. Here you will find a proliferation of small shops selling local handicrafts and Maldivian souvenirs made abroad. You will also find a selection of cosy little tearooms in this quarter.

The northern portion of Chaandanee Magu is also sometimes called the Singapore Bazaar, as many of the goods come from Singapore, one of the nearest neighbors of the Maldives. Visit Bamboo or Royal Art for batik and Lemon for colorful T-shirts and other souvenir items.

Dhoni Boats, Shark's Teeth & Maldivian Curiosities

One of the most popular crafted items sold in this shopping district is the miniature dhoni boat. Usually made from coconut wood, it is a small replica of the traditional seafaring vessel of the Maldives. It can be dismantled and re-assembled for easy transportation. Beware, though, of buying dhonis crafted from coral, as there are restrictions on the exportation of coral for environmental reasons.

You will find a large selection of the wooden variety at shops such as M Orchid Uffa, located on Faamudheyri Magu or Gloria Maris or Lemon on Chaandanee Magu. For authentic shark's teeth, another popular keepsake, check out The Shop, on Faamudheyri.

There is a Middle Eastern atmosphere to the local market of Male, which is primarily an outlet for fresh produce and local delicacies. A treat you may want to surprise your friends with, is the coconut chocolate, which is wrapped in palm leaves. You can also purchase jams and pickles to enjoy later.

Creative Arts & Crafts Training Center

Hanimaadhoo, Thiladhummathi Atoll
(Near Hanimaadhoo domestic airport)

Tourists may not realize that the bulk of handcrafted items sold in Maldives are actually imports from Indonesia, China and other nearby trade partners. The mission of the Creative Arts and Crafts Training Center is to rectify this through workshops and other activities that raise awareness of locally made goods. The initiative has also resulted in the creation of the Heritage Gift Shop, a sales outlet in Hanimaadhoo which is located in the Thiladhummathi Atoll towards the north of the Maldives island group.

Products range from pyrographic images to various styles of woodwork. One rich natural resource of the Maldives, is the coconut palm, so it should not come as too much of a surprise that some of the coconut shells are worked into functional items such as candle holders, penholders, plates and more. Pyrography can be used to make decorative portraits as well as user items such as vases. While carpentry and woodwork has been practiced in the Maldives for many generations, coconut timber was usually employed, because of its abundance.

Reed Mats of Huvadhoo

Located in the South Huvadhoo Atoll, the island Gadhdhoo is well known for the quality of its woven reed mats. They are made from locally harvested reeds, which are dyed and then woven into a variety of intricate and complex patterns. It is possible to buy the mats in the capital or at resort shops, but buying it on the islands where they are made means that you will only pay a fraction of the price.

Wooden Boxes from Thulhaadhoo

Baa Atoll

Another distinctly Maldivian curiosity is the lacquered wooden box. Meticulously shaped and hollowed out, the boxes, also referred to as "lielaa yehun", can be purchased at various shops around Male and other outlets catering to tourists, but the best place to look for them is at the source, Thulhaadhoo in the Baa Atoll, where they are made, along with other wooden items such as sticks, dishes and eating utensils.

Printed in Great Britain
by Amazon.co.uk, Ltd.,
Marston Gate.